BENJAMIN HARRISON

ENCYCLOPEDIA
of PRESIDENTS

Benjamin Harrison

Twenty-Third President of the United States

By Susan Clinton

Consultant: Charles Abele, Ph.D.
Social Studies Instructor
Chicago Public School System

 CHILDRENS PRESS ®
CHICAGO

Benjamin and Caroline Harrison

Library of Congress Cataloging-in-Publication Data

Clinton, Susan.
   Benjamin Harrison / by Susan Clinton.
      p.   cm. — (Encyclopedia of presidents)
   Summary: Examines the military and political career of the
only grandson of a president to become president himself.
   ISBN 0-516-01370-X
   1.   Harrison, Benjamin, 1833-1901—Juvenile
literature.   2.   Presidents—United States—Biography—
Juvenile literature.   3.   United States—Politics and
government—1889-1893—Juvenile literature.
   [1.   Harrison, Benjamin, 1833-1901.   2.   Presidents.]
I.   Title.   II.   Series.
E702.C57   1989
973.8'6092—dc20
[B]
[92]   89-33751
                                                   CIP
                                                   AC

Picture Acknowledgments

AP/Wide World Photos, Inc.—68, 86

The Bettmann Archive—5, 6, 8, 9, 11 (2
photos), 13 (3 photos), 14, 16, 17, 18, 19 (2
photos), 21 (2 photos), 22, 24, 25, 35, 36, 39, 40,
43, 48, 49 (bottom), 50, 53, 56, 57, 58, 61 (2
photos), 62, 63, 65, 67, 72, 73, 75 (2 photos), 77,
81, 82

Historical Pictures Service, Chicago—30, 31, 49
(top), 85, 89

Library of Congress—4, 32, 78, 80

U.S. Bureau of Printing and Engraving—2

Cover design and illustration
by Steven Gaston Dobson

President Benjamin Harrison

Table of Contents

Chapter 1

The Hero of Peachtree Creek

In May 1864, President Abraham Lincoln gathered together three Union armies, nearly 100,000 men altogether, and ordered them to chase down General Joseph E. Johnston's Confederate force of 65,000. Lincoln put General William Tecumseh Sherman in charge. Starting from Chattanooga, Tennessee, the bluecoats marched and fought their way south through Georgia, deeper and deeper into Confederate territory. They fought on days when the temperature was 100 degrees in the shade and they marched through rain, churning Georgia's red clay roads to slippery mud. By mid-July, they had advanced about 100 miles and lost 17,000 men, killed or wounded, without being able to corner Johnston's rebel army.

Johnston was good at managing safe retreats. While his Confederate troops pulled back, black slaves would already be working at their new campsite, digging trenches and building earthwork walls. Slavery, the ownership of human beings, was the issue that divided the United States into North and South and led to the Civil War.

Opposite page: Benjamin Harrison as a
brigadier general in the Civil War

A slave auction in New York City

Since colonial times, southern plantation owners had depended on slave labor to bring in the all-important cotton crop. Because slavery was well established before the American Revolution and before the U.S. Constitution was formed, southerners believed that the national government had no right to tamper with it. In fact, slave owners insisted that the federal government was obliged to uphold their property rights by chasing down and returning any escaped slaves.

$100 REWARD!

RANAWAY

From the undersigned, living on Current River, about twelve miles above Doniphan, in Ripley County, Mo., on 2nd of March, 1860, **A NEGRO MAN**, about 30 years old, weighs about 160 pounds; high forehead, with a scar on it; had on brown pants and coat very much worn, and an old black wool hat; shoes size No. 11.

The above reward will be given to any person who may apprehend this said negro out of the State; and fifty dollars if apprehended in this State outside of Ripley county, or $25 if taken in Ripley county.

APOS TUCKER.

A poster announcing a reward for a runaway slave

This demand for cooperation in hunting down slaves angered many people in the North. A growing number of northerners were abolitionists—they wanted to abolish or end slavery throughout the United States because they believed it was morally wrong for one human being to own another. But the great majority of northerners did not insist on freedom for the slaves; they were willing to tolerate slavery in the southern states where it was well established. However, they could not stomach extending slavery to the new territories in the West.

In 1858, a young Illinois lawyer summed up the struggle over slavery: "I believe this government cannot permanently endure half slave and half free.... It will become all one thing or all the other." The lawyer was Abraham Lincoln. In 1861 Lincoln was beginning his first term as president of the United States.

His presidency began in crisis. Eleven southern states had just seceded from the Union; that is, they declared themselves free of the national government and formed a new government, called the Confederate States of America. Lincoln could see that splitting the country in two would lead to destructive rivalry and encourage foreign meddling. More importantly, letting the South go would endanger America's principle of majority rule. Democracy would work only if everyone was willing to live by the vote of the majority. If the South was allowed to quit to get its way, what would prevent any other discontented section or group from declaring itself outside the law? The Union would splinter to pieces.

Lincoln could not let the South secede; to preserve the Union, he had to lead the North into the Civil War. Both sides believed that the war would be short; neither side was prepared for four years of total war. The North had the advantage of a larger population, more money, a navy, and the industrial capacity to produce uniforms, shoes, tents, and guns. But the South had a big advantage—all it had to do to win the war was to survive. No single loss on the battlefield would lose the war. On the other hand, no single victory would win it for the North. The North would have to destroy the Confederacy to win.

Above: Abraham Lincoln as a young Illinois lawyer
Below: Lincoln's first inauguration, March 4, 1861

In the summer of 1864, after three years of war, people in the North were tired of fighting and tired of President Lincoln, whom they called "the widow-maker." The only thing that would restore the voters' faith in Lincoln and the Union cause was a success on the battlefield.

North and South waited anxiously for news from Georgia. As Johnston fell back to the heavy fortifications around Atlanta, southern newspapers predicted that Sherman's army would be cut to ribbons. As Sherman neared Atlanta, northern newspapers predicted that the city would fall. Days went by; weeks went by. People on both sides became frustrated—why don't they do something? The Confederate government replaced Johnston with firebrand John Bell Hood, a general who was sure to do something. Hood loved to attack. Sherman was pleased; he was ready for a fight.

With part of his troops marching wide around Atlanta, Sherman sent another group, the Army of the Cumberland, directly south across Peachtree Creek. After a rainy summer, the creek was overflowing with rushing, muddy water. The whole army had to file, brigade by brigade, across makeshift bridges. It was an ideal moment for a Confederate attack, but no attack came. Once across the creek, the army formed a long battle line and waited.

All along the battle line the men were at ease. With their muskets stacked and ready, some built cooking fires, others rolled up for a nap; some played cards, shooing the flies and swatting at the mosquitoes that buzzed around in the midsummer heat. A few wandered over the hill just ahead of them to pick wild blackberries.

Above: Confederate general Johnston (left) and Union general Sherman (right)
Below: Confederate generals John Bell Hood (left) and Joseph Johnston (right)

Benjamin Harrison (left) with fellow army officers

Once his men were settled in the hollow alongside Peachtree Creek, Colonel Benjamin Harrison left them to have a look around. Harrison commanded the First Brigade of the Third Division in the Army of the Cumberland.

Just in front of his brigade was a hill; Harrison rode up the hillside. He knew that the Confederates were close by, close enough to send occasional bullets zinging past. At the ridge of the hill, he looked down the other side across open, grassy ground that stretched clear to the enemy lines. This open field was about a quarter of a mile wide, with scrubby woods on either side. It made a natural path for an enemy charge. This bothered Harrison because, if the Confederates did charge across the field and up the hill, they would be able to stand on the ridge and fire down on his men.

There were no Union troops guarding this open section of the hilltop. Harrison looked right and left along the ridge. Off to either side, he could make out blue uniforms in the trees and underbrush. The Union battle line extended all along the ridge of the hill—except for this quarter-mile gap directly above Harrison's men. Why couldn't his brigade move to the hilltop?

Harrison went down and checked his orders. They were firm: stay down by the creek. Suddenly one of the soldiers who had been picking blackberries came racing down the hill—the rebels were moving! They were charging in force, heading right for that quarter-mile gap in the line!

Harrison spurred his horse forward to get his brigade moving. As he did so, the first line of gray uniforms appeared on the crest of the hill. It was happening exactly as Harrison had feared. With Confederates firing down into his brigade, there was no time to wait for orders, no time to aim and fire muskets. Harrison shouted, "Come on boys, we've never been licked yet, and we won't begin now." Then he led a charge, straight up the hill into enemy fire.

At the top of the hill, the First Brigade slammed into the enemy. In the shoving mass, there was no room to shoot. Men used their guns as clubs to beat one another or stabbed each other with bayonets. Harrison pushed his horse into the thick of the fight and the First Brigade pressed on after him, fighting hand-to-hand. The graycoats kept coming, kept pushing.

Harrison's superior officer, Major General Joseph Hooker

Harrison was determined that the blue line would hold. Off to his left, he could see that some Union artillerymen had stopped firing. They were turning their cannons around to roll them down toward the creek. To them, it looked as if the Confederates were breaking through; they wanted to keep the cannons out of rebel hands. Their retreat could signal a general panic. Harrison forced his way over to their commander and shouted, "Don't be afraid. I'll take care of your guns. Turn about and put them into action again." The artillerymen obeyed.

Gradually, the Confederate charge thinned. Then the enemy soldiers retreated down the hill. The blue line had held. Harrison's foresight and bravery had helped prevent a disaster. Later that afternoon Harrison's superior, Major

General Ulysses S. Grant

General Hooker, acknowledged what Harrison had done, promising, "I'll make you a brigadier-general for this fight!" Hooker kept his promise. On March 22, 1864, Harrison was promoted to brigadier general of the Union Army.

Harrison was a conscientious and brave officer who had won the lifelong respect and loyalty of his men. In the decades following the Civil War, a man's war service remained a vivid and important part of his political identity. In the postwar period, people elected a succession of Civil War generals to the presidency—Ulysses S. Grant, Rutherford B. Hayes, and James A. Garfield. In 1888, Benjamin Harrison would become the last Civil War general to be elected president.

William Henry Harrison confronts Shawnee chief Tecumseh.

Harrison came from a military background. His grandfather, William Henry Harrison, won national fame for his victory over the Indians at Tippecanoe in 1811. Later he fought against the British and their Indian allies in the War of 1812. William Henry Harrison's military ability, combined with the simplicity of his Ohio farm life, captured the nation's imagination.

His tremendous popular appeal won him the presidency in 1840. His campaign symbols, a log cabin and a jug of cider, emphasized that Harrison was a common man, not a wealthy New Yorker like his opponent, Martin Van Buren. William Henry Harrison was just the sort of man America was proud of producing: a farmer-statesman—brave, patriotic, talented, and humble.

Top: Benjamin
Harrison's grandfather,
the popular general
William Henry
Harrison, on horseback

Bottom: Martin Van
Buren, William Henry
Harrison's opponent in
the 1840 presidential
race

Benjamin Harrison had many of his grandfather's traits, and he proved his bravery and patriotism in the Civil War. He was honest, loyal, and hardworking. He was devoted to his family and his church. But he was not exciting.

Perhaps it was his looks. Whereas William Henry Harrison had been tall and handsome, his grandson was short, about five feet, six inches tall, and stout. His manner was serious and reserved. Close friends described his blue eyes as "twinkling"; others found them piercing.

Perhaps it was his prosperity. Benjamin Harrison was a very successful lawyer. He had earned every penny himself and he generously gave much of it away, but, in general, people of his time didn't trust lawyers. Harrison himself wrote, "It has become a generally acknowledged proposition that no honest or pious man can practice law with success."

Harrison had impressive intelligence, integrity, and unselfish willingness to work. But he was never able to inspire the excitement and affection of the American public. Those who knew him well admired him, but to the masses of voters he seemed remote and cold.

Benjamin Harrison holds a strange position among American presidents. The same man, Grover Cleveland, was president before him and after him. Harrison was disappointed to serve for only one term because he knew that his policies would be overturned. But the balance and detached judgment that made him seem cold also helped Harrison to accept defeat.

For himself, Harrison wrote, defeat brings "no personal disappointments."

Above: A political barbecue, one of the typical campaign activities that helped elect Benjamin Harrison's grandfather, William Henry, to the presidency in 1840

Right: Grover Cleveland, America's twenty-second and twenty-fourth president. Benjamin Harrison, as the twenty-third president, served between Cleveland's two terms.

Chapter 2

Big Decisions

When Benjamin Harrison was a boy, he could sit on his front porch and watch flatboats float down the Ohio River. The boats were loaded with pioneer families moving their furniture, their tools, and their pigs and chickens west to settle new lands. The Harrison family's farm life in North Bend, Ohio, was much like that of other pioneer families. They raised most of their food on their own farm. A young boy like Ben had the freedom to roam the countryside, fishing, hunting ducks, swimming in the summer, and sledding in the winter, but he also had a routine of chores. Ben Harrison admitted that he was never good at milking cows, but he had a knack for making the candles that lighted the Harrisons' dining room at night.

Because there was no school nearby, the children went to school in a log cabin right on the farm. The cabin was heated by a large fireplace. On the short winter days, the Harrison children and their cousins sat on backless wooden benches reciting their lessons. Their father, John Scott Harrison, hired a teacher who lived with the family.

One of Harrison's ancestors was a Virginia settler in the 1600s, as are these men.

John Scott Harrison and his wife, Elizabeth, had eight children to educate; four others had died as infants or very young children. Benjamin, born August 20, 1833, was their second child. For five generations before him, there had been Harrisons named Benjamin. These Benjamins included an English emigrant who came to the Virginia colony in 1632. They also included young Ben's great-grandfather, who signed the Declaration of Independence and became the governor of Virginia from 1781 to 1784. Governor Harrison's second son, William Henry Harrison, was Ben's grandfather.

By the time Ben Harrison was born, General William Henry Harrison had retired from an exciting career in the army to live on his 2,800-acre farm at North Bend on the

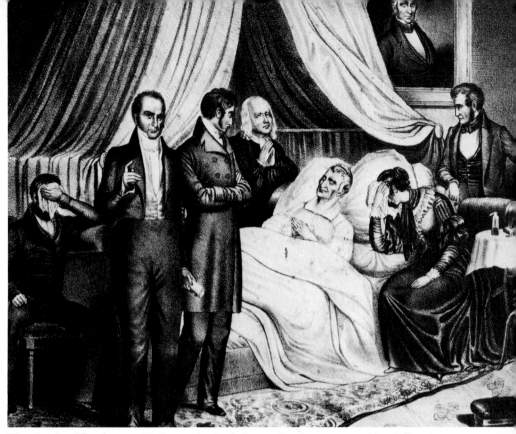

The death of Ben's grandfather, who had cheered many guests at North Bend

Ohio River. This house was open to a constant stream of visitors, many of them old soldiers who had served with the general in his campaigns. On Sundays after church, General Harrison and his wife would often entertain at their well-stocked table. On those Sundays when it was not too muddy or too snowy to travel, young Ben Harrison and his family were among the guests.

In 1840, when Ben was seven years old, his grandfather was elected president of the United States. William Henry Harrison left for Washington on a steamboat in January 1841. He was inaugurated on a bitterly cold day in March and then, one month later, died of pneumonia. The family brought his body back to be buried on his beloved land at North Bend.

Over the years when the general was away from home, running the family farm had fallen to this third son, Ben's father, John Scott Harrison. Farming so near the Ohio River was not an easy or secure life. In spring, the river often flooded the fields; in hot, dry summers it receded. Every fall, John Scott had to boat the year's harvest down the Ohio and Mississippi rivers to New Orleans and sell for the best price he could get. John Scott had given up a career in law to take over the family farm, and his father acknowledged his help by giving him the Point. This was a long, narrow, 600-acre piece of land jutting out between two rivers, the Miami on the north side and the Ohio on the south.

Although the land was fertile and John Scott worked very hard, he never made a success of the farm. Due to floods, illness, and poor decisions, he was never able to save any money. Many years found him close to bankruptcy, so that he had to borrow money to get through the year. As a boy, Ben was unaware of his father's struggles. As a man, Benjamin Harrison would contribute to the support of his father and his younger brothers and sisters all his life.

In 1847, when Ben was fourteen years old, his father somehow set aside enough money to send him and his brother Irwin to a school called Farmer's College near Cincinnati. There he had the good luck to study with a great teacher, Dr. Robert Hamilton Bishop. Bishop had been teaching history and political economy at American universities for forty years. In his classes, instead of using textbooks, he used actual government documents. The boys were required to read these documents, report on them, and discuss them.

Bishop often told the students, "Other things being equal, that man will succeed best in any given work who had the most facts." Ben took this advice to heart. Throughout his career as lawyer, soldier, senator, and president, he insisted on mastering the facts of the cases and problems before him.

Bishop also passed on a respect and love for democratic government. He believed democracy began with individual self-respect and self-control. The discipline of Farmer's College was based on Bishop's humane ideas: ". . . that every young man who wishes to be a scholar, and expects to be useful as a member of a free community, must at a very early period of life acquire the power of self-government."

Ben took this to heart, too. At Farmer's College he developed a habit of responsibility and hard work that remained with him for life.

Though Ben's studies were interrupted by trips home to help with spring planting and fall harvesting, his father managed to keep the boys enrolled at Farmer's College until Ben's mother died in the summer of 1850. This was a disastrous summer of illness for the family; two of the young children also died, three were laid up with dysentery, and Ben himself had an infected right hand. John Scott had always planned to send Ben east to Yale or Harvard, but he simply couldn't afford it. So, the fall after his mother's death, Ben set off for Miami University in Oxford, Ohio, to complete his college education.

In 1850, Miami University had 250 students, all young men, who followed the school's strict regimen. Everyone began the day with chapel services at 7:30, followed by Latin at 8:00, Greek at 9:00, and natural science at 10:00. During their midday study break, students had a chance to study or relax and read letters from home before getting back to work.

At Miami, Ben was invited to join the Union Literary Society, a debating club with its own library collection of 1,700 books. This was valuable for him because most of the university's books were chosen as reading for future ministers. The Union Literary Society, however, collected government documents and books on Harrison's favorite subjects—history, law, and politics.

Ben excelled at extemporaneous speaking, that is, speaking without advance preparation. This ability to organize a good speech at a moment's notice served Harrison well. In forty years of political life, Harrison never needed a speech writer.

Harrison's professors didn't foresee a career in politics for this sober, hardworking student; many of them hoped he would become a Presbyterian minister and put his speaking skills to use giving sermons.

Harrison had, in fact, considered the ministry. After all, he came from a religious family. His grandparents had donated money and wood to build a Presbyterian church near their home in North Bend. When Ben's own family was unable to make the trip to church services, they sang hymns and read the Bible together in the dining room at the Point. But when it came to choosing a career, he was drawn to the law. By the time he graduated in 1852, he had made two important decisions: he would look for a position in a law office, and he would marry Caroline Scott.

Across the street from the university was a boardinghouse of a young women's school, the Oxford Female Institute. Although Miami's scholars were to be in their rooms by 7:00 each night and the young women also had limited visiting hours, Benjamin had found time to go buggy-riding and sleigh-riding with charming, light-hearted Carrie Scott. Her father, John W. Scott, had founded the Female Institute. When Ben graduated, the two were secretly engaged but neither knew how long it would be before he could support a wife.

For the next two years, Ben would have to study law — not in a school, but in a Cincinnati law firm, working as an unpaid apprentice. During the day, his job consisted of copying papers for the lawyers. At night, he studied books from the firm's library. As he wrote to one of his sisters, "I suppose you have read about the Great Desert. Well, my life is as about as barren of anything funny as the Great Desert is of grass."

As he waited daily for letters from Carrie, Ben worried over when they could marry. His college roommate, John Anderson, wrote to him urging delay: "You are far from able to support Carrie as you will. You have no way to turn your mind and attainments into *cash* at present that I know of. Nor will you have for another year." Anderson's advice was practical and well-meant, but Ben decided to ignore it.

Cincinnati, Ohio, as it looked in the 1850s when Harrison lived there

First, he wanted to rescue Carrie from her situation. A young teacher and friend of Carrie's at the Female Institute was dying. Between nursing her friend, and filling in as teacher of her music and sewing classes, Carrie herself had become very ill. In addition, Ben had been living with a married sister in Cincinnati, but she and her husband were moving out of the city. Without any salary, Ben couldn't afford fifty dollars a week to stay in a boardinghouse. He would have to move back home, to the Point, to finish his studies anyway; he decided to bring a wife home with him.

The state capitol of Indiana at Indianapolis

On October 20, 1853, Benjamin and Carrie were married in her father's front room. Ben wore a sober, black frock coat and she dressed in a gray traveling suit. After a simple ceremony, the couple went to the Point where they would live with Ben's family for six months. Ben traveled back and forth to Cincinnati, borrowing books and bringing homework. In 1854, he passed the bar exam, which enabled him to set up business as a lawyer. But where?

Ben Harrison did not want to stay too close to home. In Cincinnati, where his family was so well known, he was afraid people would always think of him as a boy. Instead he and Carrie chose Indianapolis, a growing city that had room, Ben hoped, for a hardworking young lawyer.

Chapter 3

Getting Started

In 1854, Indianapolis was a rapidly growing city but not a very sophisticated one. Its population had quadrupled from 4,000 in 1847 to 16,000 in 1854. A foreign visitor noticed how friendly and how unfashionable the folks in Indianapolis were: "Workmen appeared in their blouses or dusty coats, just as they came from the workshop; farmers stepped in high boots. And yet this incongruous mass did not behave unbecomingly. Had they but shaken hands less violently! I yet feel western cordiality in my stiff arm."

The railroad, which made it easier to sell goods in other cities, had changed Indianapolis from a farmer's market town to a manufacturing and business center. New businesses in Indianapolis made chairs, barrels, wool, cloth, carriages, and steam engines. In the midst of all this bustle, people lived simply, tending kitchen gardens, fishing the river, and hunting just outside the city for deer and wild turkeys. Social life centered around churchgoing; business success depended on knowing people.

Ben Harrison was twenty-one, but with his light hair and his short, slender frame, he looked younger. He did know one family in Indianapolis; Ben's cousin William Sheets was a well-to-do paper manufacturer there. Sheets did his best to introduce Ben to other businessmen, but cases came in very slowly for the newcomer.

At first Harrison depended on a clerical job announcing court cases for $2.50 a day. His break came when the county prosecuting attorney asked Harrison to help him in a burglary trial. This was Harrison's first trial. It dragged on through the afternoon and into the evening. All afternoon Harrison took pages and pages of notes. Since the prosecuting attorney could not be there at the evening sessions, he left Harrison in charge of their closing argument. Harrison was arguing against David Wallace, a former governor of Indiana and a well-respected lawyer.

In the evening, the court was lit by candles, two on the judge's desk, two on the clerk's table, a few mounted on the walls, and one on Harrison's table. The light was so dim that, no matter how he shifted the paper, Harrison could not read a word of his notes. After a moment of panic, Harrison gave up on the notes and began to speak from memory. He did a good job and won the case. More importantly, he won the respect of Governor Wallace.

In March 1855, Governor Wallace's son, William, invited Harrison to become his law partner. William Wallace was ready to go into politics but he did not want to give up his prosperous law practice. He asked Harrison to step in and handle his cases while he was campaigning. Harrison accepted gladly; Wallace's name pulled in clients

A typical law office, where young lawyers both lived and worked

and gave Harrison a chance to prove himself. This was just the boost Harrison needed. By the time the partners separated six years later, Harrison was firmly established.

During these years, Harrison decided to go into politics himself. His family traditionally belonged to the Whig Party, but in the 1850s, the conflict between North and South over slavery was reshaping political parties. The Whig Party was splintering and dissolving; Whig candidates won fewer and fewer votes as the slavery issue heated up. The Democratic Party stood for a restrained federal government and strong state governments. Democrats defended the right of southern states to own slaves and the right of new territories to decide for themselves whether they would allow slavery or not.

Oliver Perry Morton

The new Republican Party sprang up in 1854 to oppose allowing slavery in the new territories of Kansas and Nebraska. Most Republicans were not abolitionists—they were not in favor of ending slavery throughout the South. Oliver Perry Morton, Indiana's first Republican governor, stated, "Our creed is plain. We do not assail slavery where it exists entrenched behind legal enactments, but wherever it sallies forth, we are pledged to meet it as an enemy of mankind." They called themselves antislavery men; Democrats called them "Black Republicans."

John Scott Harrison thought the Republicans were a fanatical party, determined to bring on a war. But when Ben Harrison came to choose his party, he went Republican. In 1857, he became a Republican candidate for city attorney of Indianapolis and won. In 1860, he ran for Indiana supreme court reporter, a job that entailed recording all the trials and decisions of the state supreme court in book form. The positions Harrison chose to run for would not bring him power or glamour. The supreme court reporter's job was routine and burdensome. But it was a way to find out how politics worked, a way to meet the powerful politicians in his state, and a way to put his name before the voters.

Every candidate on the Republican ticket was expected to "stump" the state. This meant traveling from town to town, usually by horse and buggy, ready to jump on a tree stump and speak anywhere they could draw a crowd. In reality, Harrison didn't have to stand on tree stumps. For the small towns in Indiana, politics was entertainment. Party workers built speakers' platforms and decorated them with red, white, and blue. They organized picnics and rallies, courthouse meetings, and torchlight parades where the candidates could speak. People rode in from their farms to listen, and they were willing to listen for hours.

In one town, Harrison planned to challenge a speech by the Democratic candidate for governor, Thomas Hendricks. He had clipped a copy of Hendricks's speech and glued it in his notebook so he could refer to it. But once he was on the platform, he opened his notebook only to find that the clipping had fallen out. Harrison made a joke out of it: he said he had proved that not a single word Hendricks said would stick!

One evening when Harrison arrived in the little country town of Rockville, he found that Thomas Hendricks was speaking there the same day. Hendricks proposed a joint meeting. Harrison accepted even though, as he put it, "Mr. Hendricks is at the head of the Democratic ticket, while I am at the tail of the Republican ticket." So many people jammed into the courthouse that Harrison had to sit on the edge of a desk, his feet dangling off the floor, while Hendricks spoke for four hours. Then Hendricks courteously asked the crowd to hear out his opponent.

Harrison took the floor and began answering Hendricks point by point. As he spoke, audience enthusiasm soared. One Rockville resident said, "Such a drubbing as the little fellow did give them! And he was so clean about it! No abuse, no blackguarding! I would walk a hundred miles to see it done over." The story was told all over the state; Harrison was no longer an unknown.

Harrison won the election for court reporter. In the fall of 1860, Indiana went Republican, electing a Republican governor and giving its electoral votes to the Republican presidential candidate, Abraham Lincoln. With the election of a "Black Republican" for president, the southern states were angry and alarmed, even though Lincoln had repeatedly promised not to interfere with slavery in the South. One Georgia newspaper wrote, "Let the consequences be what they may — whether the Potomac is crimsoned in human gore, and Pennsylvania Avenue is paved ten fathoms deep with mangled bodies . . . the South will never submit to such humiliation and degradation as the inauguration of Abraham Lincoln."

Union troops defending Fort Sumter

Before Lincoln was inaugurated, South Carolina,
Mississippi, Florida, Alabama, Georgia, Louisiana, and
Texas had formally left the Union. Lincoln took office on
March 4, 1861. On April 12, southern guns opened fire on
United States troops at Fort Sumter, South Carolina. After
thirty-three hours under fire, the Union commander sur-
rendered and the Confederate flag was raised above the
fort. The Civil War had begun.

Chapter 4

Fighting Confederates
and Copperheads

On April 5, 1861, President Lincoln asked Governor Morton of Indiana to enlist 6,000 volunteers for the Union Army. Morton sent 12,000. The North was on fire with patriotism. Ministers were preaching Union; newspapers, both Democratic and Republican, were all for war against the rebellious South. As volunteers swarmed to Indianapolis, there were parades and demonstrations in their honor. Through it all, Harrison worked steadily away, spending days at his busy law office and any spare time in a rented basement office putting together the records of the supreme court.

Since moving to Indianapolis, he and Carrie had had two children—Russell, born August 12, 1854, and Mary, born April 3, 1858. One of Ben's younger brothers and one of his nephews had also come to live with the family. The Harrisons had been renting a little wooden house with three rooms, a bedroom, a dining room, and a kitchen. With six people to house and support, Harrison needed a bigger house. He bought one, a two-story house with a stable, for one thousand dollars. Paying for the house added to Harrison's worries about supporting his family. He reluctantly held back from enlisting.

At the beginning of the Civil War, northern enthusiasm was so great that Harrison truly felt he was not needed in the war effort. But by July 1862, a combination of military defeats and a growing list of men killed and wounded had cooled northern enthusiasm. When Lincoln called for more troops, very few men volunteered.

In July 1862, Governor Morton of Indiana confided to Harrison that he couldn't get enough men to meet his state quota. Harrison immediately volunteered to go himself and to convince a company of volunteers to go with him. Harrison hung a flag out of his office window, hired a drummer and a fife-player to provide marching music for his future company, and started on another round of stump-speaking, this time for the Union Army.

By the end of July, Harrison had enlisted eighty-five men who would form the A Company in the 70th Regiment of Indiana Infantry Volunteers. Governor Morton named Harrison a colonel of the new regiment. Harrison hired a drillmaster to start turning these farmers, store-owners, and businessmen into soldiers and arranged for his law partners to help his family. When the new regiment got its orders to move, the city gave them a warm send-off. After four dress parades, an evening of speeches, and lots of cheering, Harrison's regiment left home on a train for Louisville, Kentucky, on August 13, 1862.

In the next year and a half, the 70th would have more than enough time to drill. They were assigned to guard duty, protecting trains and railroad tracks. During these dull months, Harrison spent his days trying to maintain discipline and morale among his men. He spent his eve-

An antislavery meeting in Boston, Massachusetts

nings in his tent studying the art of war. Over and over, he requested that the 70th go to the front; meanwhile, he believed that "every day in camp should be used in prep-- aration for that other day, always to be kept in mind—the day of battle."

By 1864 the Union seemed no closer to winning the war than it had been in 1861. Moreover, Lincoln's Emancipation Proclamation of 1862 was not well received in the North. This declared that all slaves in rebelling states would be free as of January 1, 1863. Though they did not like slavery, most northerners were not ready to accept black people as equals. Antiwar Democrats, called Copperheads, were claiming that Lincoln was controlled by the abolitionists. They campaigned for an end to the fighting and a negotiated peace with the Confederacy.

Some of the Copperheads went beyond criticism into outright treason. They formed secret organizations called Sons of Liberty and Knights of the Golden Circle, dedicated to overthrowing the government. They planned to take over the western states of Illinois, Indiana, Ohio, Missouri, and Kentucky and break away from the Union to form a Northwestern Confederacy. In Indiana, Sons of Liberty leaders claimed to have between 75,000 and 125,000 members. Five of their leaders were found guilty of conspiracy and sentenced to life imprisonment by a military court.

Not all Democrats were Sons of Liberty; many were loyal citizens who objected to the great expansion of government power during the war. Some objected to the military draft, some to the emancipation of the slaves, and some to the use of the military to keep peace in troubled northern states. Many Democrats were simply disillusioned with the war and its tremendous cost in money, resources, and human life.

In Indiana, Democrats won control of the legislature and replaced Harrison with a Democratic court reporter. Losing his post made Harrison angry, but he was even angrier about a Copperhead letter campaign that urged his men to desert the army and stop fighting in a wrong-headed Republican war.

Finally, in February 1864, the 70th was ordered into the war. They marched south to join General Sherman's force. On the march, heavy rains soaked the men and their bedding. At night, the sodden blankets froze. Mules wore out pulling wagons through the deep mud and fell dead on the road. The 70th was not the first regiment to lose its animals this way. Harrison described one day's march along a road "lined with dead mules and horses and the stench was sickening. . . . We got our water for coffee out of a creek in the morning; and when we started to march up it, found dead mules in and along the creek at the rate of a hundred to a mile. We joked it off, however, as only soldiers can, and suffered no detriment from our cups of mule tea."

Once the 70th joined up with Sherman, they continued south, chasing General Johnston and his Confederates from one set of fortifications to another. All across the North people complained about Sherman's slowness to attack. Down in Georgia, Harrison wrote about the fortifications an attacker would have to get through: first, there would be a tangle of trees cut down in a jumbled pile; then, farther on, a row of cut treetops with all their branches sharpened.

If a soldier got within twenty yards of the rifle pits, he would be stopped by a double line of sharpened stakes, set close together and buried deep in the ground at one end, with the sharp ends pointed right at him. Finally, he would have to climb an earth wall and jump down on the men inside. Of course, anyone trying to hack through these obstacles would be working under constant enemy musket fire. Harrison wrote, "I should like to see a few thousand of the 'On To Atlanta' civilians of the North charging such a line of works. Most of the tender-skin[n]ed individuals of this class would require help to get into the works if they were *empty*."

In this Atlanta campaign, Harrison would fight more battles than his grandfather, William Henry Harrison, fought in his entire life. His first battle was at Resaca, Georgia, on May 15, 1864. Harrison's brigade was to storm a Confederate gun battery on top of a hill. At a run, Harrison led his men down a hillside, through a dense pine grove, and up the enemy's hill straight into enemy gunfire. In the first half hour, 250 of his men were killed. At the top, they poured over the earth wall and fought the artillerymen hand-to-hand. Sherman called it "handsome fighting."

After Resaca, Harrison's men nicknamed him "Little Ben." It was a sign of their trust in him. One soldier recalled that the men were "glad to fight by the side of 'Little Ben,' who shirked nothing, and took just the same chance of getting a bullet through the heart as we did."

At New Hope Church, on May 26, Harrison's men held their line in the face of heavy fire from Confederate trenches only three hundred yards away. Shells from enemy guns shattered the trees around them and sent splinters of wood flying. At nightfall, Harrison discovered that there were no doctors to care for his wounded men. He had some tents torn into strips for bandages and did the best he could to clean and wrap his soldiers' wounds until the doctors arrived several hours later.

At Gilgal Church in mid-June, Harrison and his regiment lay in a trench filled with puddles, firing away until they ran out of ammunition and had to pull back. At Peachtree Creek, Harrison and his men saved the day. Finally, on September 2, 1864, they were part of the jubilant Union army that marched into Atlanta. The next day, Harrison was on a train home for Indianapolis. Governor Morton had requested his help in Indiana.

Morton had two jobs waiting for Harrison. One was to campaign for Republican candidates and the other was to enlist new soldiers for the Union Army. Harrison was fresh from the front and angry with those who stayed safely at home and complained about the war. Campaigning gave Harrison a chance to speak his mind about Copperheads and prejudice: "Not a negro has escaped and made his way into our camps but has brought more aid to our cause than the entire brood of whining, carping Copperheads who object, in the interest of treason, to the employment of the black men."

Sherman's capture of Atlanta and a Union victory at Cedar Creek in the Shenandoah Valley cheered the North and deflated the Copperheads. Morton was reelected governor and Harrison was reelected court reporter. In the national elections, Lincoln won a landslide victory.

The day after Lincoln's reelection, Harrison took a train south to Atlanta to rejoin Sherman, but the train never made it. About twenty miles into Georgia, the tracks had been torn up. As a result, a jumble of Union regiments was stranded. Harrison was put in command of a brigade and sent to Nashville, Tennessee, to help hold that city against Confederate General Hood and his army. In two days of fighting, Hood was driven out. Harrison was free to make another try at rejoining Sherman. On his way to New York to catch a steamer to the South, Harrison caught scarlet fever and had to spend several weeks recovering.

Lincoln's assassin, John Wilkes Booth, dashes from the scene of the crime.

By now he had been promoted to brigadier general. Harrison took the steamer again, reached a recruiting camp on the South Carolina coast, and spent weeks drilling new troops through swarms of gnats and mosquitoes. Before Harrison could rejoin his brigade, the Confederates had surrendered. On April 19, 1865, Harrison finally reached Sherman's army and his own headquarters. But no one came forward to welcome Little Ben back. The troops had just learned that Abraham Lincoln had been assassinated. General Harrison's first job on his return was to speak at a memorial service for Lincoln.

Sherman's army made a last trek to Washington, D.C., to march in the Grand Review, a two-day parade celebrating the end of the war. On June 8, 1865, Harrison was officially discharged from the army. When he arrived in Indianapolis two days later, he found he was a war hero.

Above: The battle of Resaca, Georgia, where Harrison fought boldly
Below: Atlanta, Georgia, after Union troops captured it

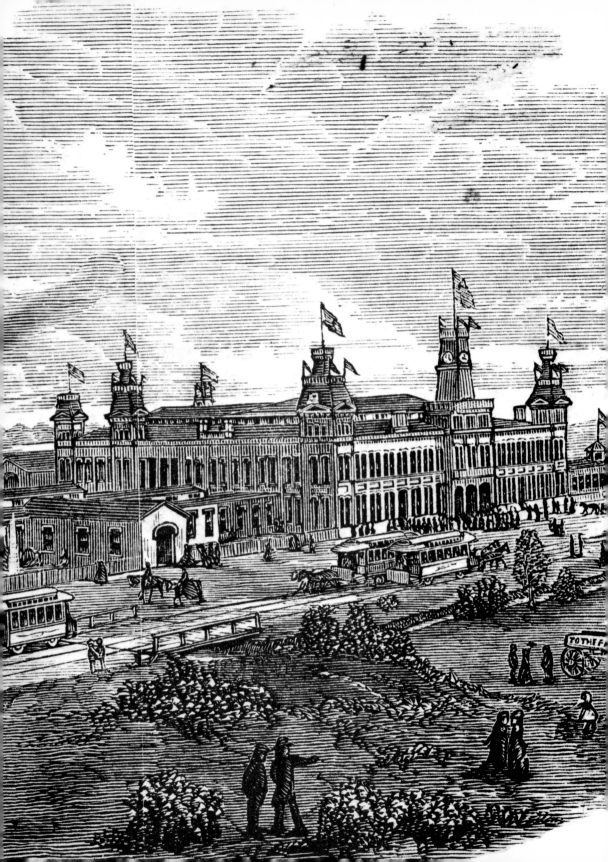

Chapter 5

Biding His Time

As Harrison settled back into work at his firm, he became involved in a sensational case that kept his name before the public. This case brought back all the bitter feelings of the Civil War. During the war, General Alvin Hovey had arrested Lambdin Milligan, an Indiana lawyer and a leader in the Sons of Liberty, for conspiring against the government. Milligan was convicted by a military court, sentenced to life imprisonment, and put to work in the prison paint shop.

In 1866, the U.S. Supreme Court freed Milligan. It ruled that no military court had the right to try civilians in peaceful territory where there were adequate civilian courts. Two years later, in 1868, Milligan sued the military officers who arrested and tried him; he had gotten lead poisoning from the prison paint shop and he wanted $100,000 to make up for the loss of his health.

President Ulysses S. Grant appointed Harrison to defend General Hovey and the others; Milligan's lawyer was Harrison's old political foe, Democrat Thomas Hendricks. Every day people crowded into the courtroom to watch the trial, and newspapers reported on its progress. Legally, Milligan was in the right. But people were angered at the idea that a traitor would go free and then be paid a huge sum of money. Harrison used the trial to bring out the whole story of the Indiana Sons of Liberty. He had witnesses describe their plan to let five thousand Confederate prisoners loose in Indianapolis to terrorize the city, seize the capital, and set up a state government sympathetic to the Confederacy.

In contrast, he conjured up a picture of the sacrifices made by Union soldiers and their loyal families: "And how many houses there were in which lonely wives and fatherless little ones dragged wearily on, their days and nights full of painful watching and apprehension . . . when sickness came, and the child stretched upon the bed, moaning and tossing with fever, asked with parched lips for papa, and when he would come home."

Hendricks accused Harrison of inflaming the minds of the jury. That is exactly what Harrison was doing, but he had a good answer: "If you have felt your hearts kindled with an honest indignation, what did it except the simple narration of the facts? I pity the heart, I pity the man that can listen to such stories of wrong, conspiracy, and treason, and not find his heart all aglow with honest indignation." Harrison's appeal reached the jury. Instead of the $100,000 Milligan sued for, they awarded him only $5.

Godlove Orth

In 1876, Harrison's friends wanted to nominate him for governor. Harrison firmly refused. The Indiana Republican Party was controlled by Oliver Morton, who had been the Civil War governor of Indiana. Now a U.S. senator, Morton did not want to support a man who could become his own rival for power. Harrison's father summed up the situation. "In a *private* position he cannot injure your claims for higher honor. In a *candidacy* he has you in the slaughter house of his friends."

Harrison stuck to his decision not to run; the Republicans chose Godlove Orth, a prominent Republican who was serving as foreign minister to Austria. Though Grant himself was an honest and straightforward man, he placed his trust in weak, corrupt men. Many of his appointees used their power to enrich themselves at the people's expense. Newspapers in Washington and then in Indiana began to expose Godlove Orth as one of them.

Since the Civil War, Republicans had been able to stay in power by "waving the bloody shirt." That is, they would whip up bitter memories of the Civil War and remind people that the Republicans had fought for the Union while the Democrats were the party of rebellious slaveholders. But the corruption of the Grant administration disgusted even loyal Republicans. In Indiana, support for Orth was melting away.

In August, Harrison returned from a month-long fishing trip to find that Orth had resigned his candidacy. Harrison was met at the train station by five thousand cheering supporters. They urged him to step in as the Republican candidate for governor. Harrison accepted. His Democratic opponent was James D. Williams, better known as "Blue Jeans Williams" for his habit of wearing overalls. Democrats called Harrison "Kid Gloves Harrison" and accused him of being cold and aristocratic.

Harrison did wear gloves—not for fashion's sake, but to protect a hand that had been infected years earlier. While Williams stirred up anger over Republican corruption, Harrison "waved the bloody shirt" at soldiers' reunions. One Republican campaign song ran:

> The Boys in Blue and soldiers true
> Are shouting loud for General Ben.
> While from the river to the lakes
> He draws a host of loyal men.
> But nowhere in the Hoosier State
> A single voice or vote he gains
> From Copperheads or ex-Confeds
> For they all march with Uncle James.

The issue that finally decided the election was greenbacks. During the Civil War the government issued paper dollars, called greenbacks, and promised that they could be exchanged for gold dollars after the war. The problem was that a greenback dollar was no longer worth as much as a gold dollar.

Indiana farmers who had borrowed greenbacks didn't want to pay back in gold because they would end up paying back more than they borrowed. They wanted the government to declare by fiat, or order, that the greenbacks could stand on their own with no promise of eventual payment in gold. They formed their own party called the Greenbackers.

Harrison believed that it was important to back up paper money with gold. Otherwise, no one could be certain of the value of anything. The uncertainty would bring banking, business, and trade to a standstill and, in the end, hurt farmers and laborers most of all.

Harrison gave an amusing interpretation of the situation. "The greenback," he explained, "contains a promise to pay dollars. . . . And its value is measured by your faith and your neighbor's faith that the promise will be kept. The 'fiat' dollar is to contain no promise to pay, but in its stead we are to have a 'fiat' or proclamation. It would run in its simplest form thus: 'This is a dollar.' . . . Or for the pious it might read: 'In God we trust to make this a dollar,' and the holder would mentally add: 'For He only can.' For it is certain that nothing short of the 'fiat' of Him who made the world from nothing can make such a bit of paper worth one hundred cents."

A mob sacks a Pittsburgh freight yard during the 1877 railroad riots.

Harrison's position was logical, but so many Republicans deserted their own party to vote for the Greenbackers that Harrison lost the election by five thousand votes. But even though Harrison lost, he had the gratitude of Indiana Republicans for his willingness to jump in after Orth resigned.

In 1877, railroad workers across the country went on strike to protest a cut in wages. In Indianapolis, striking workers took over the station and stopped all trains. Governor Blue Jeans Williams was afraid to lose labor votes, so he waited. Harrison and other Republican leaders organized a citizens' militia to protect the city from mob

Local militia fire upon a mob during the railroad strike.

violence. Then Harrison formed a committee to hear the strikers' complaints. After two days of talk, Harrison agreed that the strikers were right about wages, but he also urged them to break off the strike. The Indianapolis strike ended without bloodshed.

In 1880, the Republican Party swept back into power in Indiana. When Harrison told friends that he would like to run for the U.S. Senate, the party nominated him unanimously. Before the Seventeenth Amendment was passed in 1913, senators were elected by the state legislatures instead of by the people. Since the Indiana legislature had a Republican majority, Harrison was easily elected.

Chapter 6

From the Senate to
the White House

One of Harrison's first duties as senator from Indiana was to interview a seemingly endless crowd of office-seekers from his home state. Harrison was well liked by the new president, James Garfield, and was able to steer some job appointments to Indiana friends.

Ever since the days of Andrew Jackson, political office brought with it control of many government jobs, called civil service jobs. When Jackson Democrats came into power, they rewarded their loyal supporters with government jobs. This meant immediately replacing Republican government workers, from ambassadors down to postmasters, with Democrats. Whenever Republicans were in office, they threw out Democratic officeholders and appointed other Republicans.

Jackson's idea was that the people had voted for a certain party because they wanted that party to run the government. In some cases, this made sense. An ambassador, for example, should share the views and carry out the policies of the president. But many thousands of civil service jobs, such as secretaries or postmasters, were routine jobs that had nothing to do with national policy. The frequent turnover made no sense at all; in fact, it led to inefficiency and corruption. Politicians rewarded their friends without worrying about who would do the best job.

Reformers urged that civil service jobs be separated from politics. They wanted the government to look for the best workers and then keep them in their jobs. Both parties talked about reform but neither was ready to give up their patronage, that is, their control of these appointed jobs. After all, patronage helped cement party loyalties.

It seemed to Harrison that anybody who had ever voted for him now felt entitled to a job. Harrison was not a reformer; he wanted to steer more federal jobs to Republicans. But he also wanted to appoint qualified people to these jobs. He wrote to a friend, "It is very distressing business to me—this attempt to furnish places for those who deserve them, when the places won't go around."

On July 2, 1881, four months after he took office, President Garfield was shot by a disappointed office-seeker named Charles Guiteau. Harrison remembered Guiteau: "He used to accost me every day about his prospects and was really a nuisance." Garfield's doctors could not find the bullet, and after two months he died. Vice-President Chester A. Arthur became president.

Above: Charles Guiteau shoots President Garfield in a Washington train station.
Below: The wounded Garfield is placed in an ambulance cart.

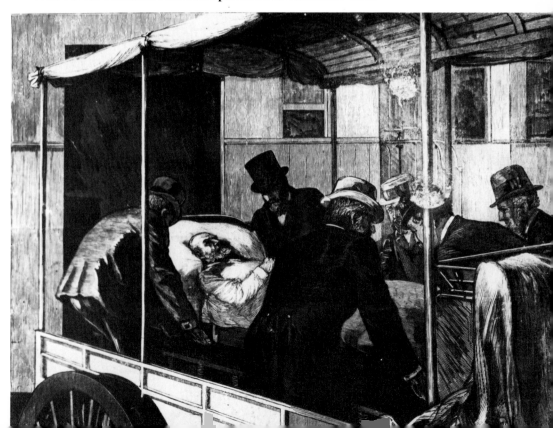

Judge Walter Q. Gresham

Arthur abruptly ended one of Harrison's patronage problems by appointing Judge Walter Q. Gresham as Indiana postmaster general. Gresham was a bitter enemy of Harrison's; he had wanted Harrison's Senate seat for himself. Gresham would now control patronage in Indiana.

During his Senate years, Harrison worked hard. He wrote to a cousin, "I am born to be a drudge." As in his law practice, he prepared his positions carefully and then defended them well, but political battles were harder to win than courtroom battles.

Harrison had a chance at the Republican presidential nomination in 1884, but his chances were spoiled by Gresham, who was competing for the nomination himself. Without unanimous support from his home state, Harrison withdrew his name. The election of 1884 was a disaster for

President Grover Cleveland

the Republicans. Grover Cleveland beat the Republican candidate, James G. Blaine, to become the first Democratic president since before the Civil War. Cleveland's vice-president was none other than Thomas Hendricks, Harrison's old rival from Indiana. In Indiana, Democrats won control of the state legislature. Harrison knew he would not be reelected to the Senate.

Toward the end of his Senate term, Harrison began carefully preparing a case against President Cleveland. Although Cleveland had changed thousands of patronage jobs to appointments based on the merit system, he had removed five hundred Republicans from civil service jobs during his first year in office. In many cases, the charges against the dismissed workers were secret and the employees had no chance to defend themselves.

Harrison collected names and dates. On March 27, 1886, he opened fire, reading a pathetic letter from a Democratic war widow who had been ousted from her post office job. She wrote, "War, with its natural and inevitable results, struck down my husband, my protector and support . . . but that the Government, to preserve which he sacrificed his life, should connive with secret enemies and false witnesses to strike down his family without an opportunity of vindication is a national disgrace, and an act too cowardly and base."

The Democrats had to reply to Harrison's powerful speech. Newspapers reprinted it and congressmen ordered and distributed over twenty thousand copies. Harrison was becoming a national Republican spokesman. Then, in 1887, Cleveland gave Harrison the issue that would make him a president.

Cleveland announced that he wanted to lower tariffs. A tariff is an extra charge or tax on goods from foreign countries. It is imposed so that the foreign goods will not be cheaper than American-made goods. Cleveland saw tariffs as a source of corruption. In his eyes, the federal government was helping American business by raising prices for American consumers. Harrison held the opposite view. He thought of the tariff as a protection for American labor. After all, foreign goods were cheaper because wages for foreign laborers were so much lower. Protecting American business kept up the wages of American laborers. The tariff became the big issue in the election of 1888.

As the Republicans cast about for a candidate, Harrison's name came up again. As a spokesman for the tariff,

A political cartoon during the tariff controversy

Harrison had the support of wealthy businessmen and bankers. In spite of Gresham's efforts against him, Harrison also had his home state solidly behind him this time. Indiana sent ten thousand Harrison supporters to the Republican convention in Chicago. They steadily worked to persuade other delegates to support Harrison.

Behind the scenes, some candidates were busy buying convention votes. Others were ready to promise away powerful government positions in exchange for convention votes. Senator Matt Quay, the political boss of Pennsylvania, quietly negotiated to give Harrison the vote of his state delegation in exchange for putting a Pennsylvanian in the president's cabinet. Harrison simply responded "No." Harrison had given his campaign workers firm instructions, "Make no promises for me."

There was only one man who could easily have won the Republican nomination in 1888, and that was James Blaine. But on the first day of the convention, Blaine sent a letter firmly refusing to run. The Republicans then had to choose among nine candidates, including Harrison and his enemy, Walter Gresham. On the first ballot, no one had a majority. But Harrison began to gather votes, first from the disappointed Blaine supporters, then from New York. He finally won the nomination on the eighth ballot.

Back in Indianapolis, Harrison got the news by telegraph in his office. By the time he got home, hundreds of people were waiting in front of his house for a speech. This was the beginning of Harrison's front-porch campaign. Almost every day, the train would bring a crowd to see Harrison and he would step out on his porch, greet them, and give a speech. One day he made seven speeches. Harrison workers made sure that his speeches made newspapers all over the country. Harrison spoke to crowds of Union veterans about pensions; he spoke to a group of black men about progress in civil rights; on July 4, 1888, he greeted ninety-one members of the Tippecanoe Club, all veterans who had voted for his grandfather in 1840. To everyone, Harrison spoke about the benefits of the tariff.

The day before the election, a giant "campaign ball" finally reached Indianapolis. This thousand-pound, red-and-white ball was forty-two feet around. As a campaign stunt, Republicans had been rolling the ball from Maryland, through Delaware, New Jersey, New York, Pennsylvania, West Virginia, and Ohio. If Harrison won, they would roll it to Washington, D.C.

An adoring crowd hails Harrison as the new president.

On election day, Harrison voted, then went home to his library to wait for the results with his family and close friends. The vote was close. Across the whole country, Cleveland got 90,000 more popular votes than Harrison. However, state by state, Harrison won more electoral votes, beating Cleveland 233 to 168. Benjamin Harrison had been elected the twenty-third president of the United States.

Chapter 7

Taking Command

On April 29, 1889, President Harrison was rowed into New York City on a ceremonial barge to preside over three days of extravagant parades, fireworks, speech-making, and banquets. One hundred years before, George Washington had been inaugurated as the first president of the United States. Now Harrison, not quite two months into his presidency, stood in Washington's place at a three-day national celebration.

Harrison began his presidency confidently. He was a Republican president backed up by a Republican majority in both houses of Congress. Harrison would have a better chance than many presidents of turning his programs into laws. Some people expected that he would let himself be ruled by more experienced politicians, such as James G. Blaine. Blaine did become Harrison's secretary of state. Contrary to Blaine's expectations, however, Harrison did not consult him about the rest of the cabinet or invite any Blaine supporters to be in it. Other powerful Republicans who had helped elect Harrison, like Matt Quay of Pennsylvania and Thomas Platt of New York, let Harrison know which cabinet posts they themselves hoped to hold. These party bosses were unpleasantly surprised when Harrison avoided them altogether in forming his cabinet.

Opposite page: Harrison (with the long beard)
on his rainy inauguration day, March 4, 1889

Harrison was not trying to ignore the Republican Party. He knew that voters did not have the strong feeling for him that they had had for leaders such as Ulysses S. Grant or his own grandfather. He knew that his election was a result of hard work, ample funds, and good organization. But along with his party loyalty, he had a very strong sense of the personal moral responsibility that came with the presidency.

When Quay, Pennsylvania party leader and national party chairman, went to Indianapolis to congratulate Harrison on his election, Harrison said, "Providence has given us the victory." Exasperated by Harrison's appointments, Quay later declared, "He ought to know that Providence hadn't a damn thing to do with it." He added that Harrison "would never know how close a number of men were compelled to approach the penitentiary to make him President."

Quay was talking about the common practice of buying votes. Both parties reserved money to bribe uncommitted voters, called floaters. In fact, a week before Harrison's election, newspapers printed a letter from the national treasurer of the Republican Party that said, "Divide the floaters into blocks of five and put a trusted man with necessary funds in charge of these five and make him responsible that none get away and that all vote our ticket."

Harrison managed to stay detached from this scandal, however. Eventually, voters were convinced that whatever the party organization was willing to do, Harrison himself remained a man of integrity.

Once the cabinet was selected, Harrison had some 1,700 other patronage jobs to fill. He refused to pass this responsibility to anyone else. He was determined to make up his own mind. Senators who expected Harrison to simply okay the names they suggested were disappointed. Harrison wanted personal information about each name on the list.

Not all of Harrison's appointments turned out well. For example, as commissioner of pensions, he chose Corporal James R. Tanner, a Civil War hero who had lost both of his legs in battle.

Tanner was a very popular choice. Harrison fully expected and wanted Tanner to be generous in awarding pensions to Civil War veterans. The president put a high value on wartime service and had always kept up ties to his own 70th regiment. Besides, with a surplus in the U.S. treasury, the country could afford pensions. But Tanner carried his duties too far. He let his Pension Bureau employees award each other big pensions. Tanner publicly stated that he would "drive a six-mule team through the Treasury" to give veterans more money. Tanner had become a public embarrassment. Finally, he was persuaded to resign.

Veterans protested; they felt they had lost an advocate. But in June 1890, Harrison signed a pension bill with more generous terms than even Tanner would have granted. For the first time, the government provided pensions for the widows, orphaned children, and dependent parents of slain veterans. After the passage of this bill, government pension spending rose from $81 million to $135 million a year.

An 1889 cartoon captioned, "Put your application in the slot and get an office"

For the first eighteen months of his presidency, Harrison interviewed job-seekers between four and six hours a day. Although he was determined to do this job properly, Harrison made no effort to do it pleasantly. The president did not invite applicants to sit down during their interviews. He often drummed his fingers impatiently while they talked. He did not offer much comfort to those who received no jobs. He would simply write, "Embarrassments are very thick and offices are very thin."

Job-seekers went home and told their friends what a cold, unfriendly man the president was. Harrison's conscientious independence was already costing him support and loyalty within his own party.

The Dakotas knock for admission to the Union.

Harrison would need solid Republican support to get anything he wanted through Congress. During Harrison's administration, South Dakota and five other western territories—North Dakota, Washington, Montana, Wyoming, and Idaho—became states, more than during any other president's term. All of these states elected Republicans to Congress. However, the new western states would not vote with their party unless the government treasury would accept silver as well as gold to back up paper money. Silver mining was a big business in the West. Having the government purchase their silver would bring in a great deal of money.

Harrison didn't mind buying silver for the treasury—it was a precious metal. However, he hesitated to circulate silver dollars because an ounce of silver was much less valuable than an ounce of gold. He feared that people wouldn't have much confidence in a silver dollar. He knew that foreign countries wouldn't accept it. Nevertheless, here were these western congressmen, with enough votes to block all the laws Harrison wanted to pass. Harrison compromised in the Sherman Silver Purchase Act: the government would buy four-and-a-half million ounces of silver every month, but it did not actually have to circulate silver coins. This compromise became law July 14, 1890. For the moment, at least, Harrison won the support of the western Republicans.

Republicans had come into power during the furor over the tariff issue. Harrison and the Republican leaders in Congress wanted to pass a new, higher tariff, and Senator William McKinley of Ohio wrote a new tariff bill. There were two obstacles. First, Harrison wanted the bill to give the president the power to adjust tariff rates in treaties with foreign countries. Harrison and Blaine called this idea "reciprocity." It meant that, if a foreign country agreed to drop its tariffs on American goods, the United States would do the same in return. Harrison saw reciprocity as a way of expanding the market for American products. Secretary of State Blaine worked on winning over the public with a newspaper campaign while Harrison worked behind the scenes, meeting with influential senators and representatives. Finally they succeeded; a reciprocity provision was written into the tariff bill.

Top: A political cartoon captioned, "Will somebody show Uncle Sam how to see through the silver trouble?"

Bottom: An 1896 cartoon illustrating the Democrats' stand on the silver issue

I AM SILVER BLIND PLEASE ASSIST ME

SILVERITE

SOUND MONEY DEMOCRATS

DEM. PARTY

ABYSS OF POLITICAL MANIA

In the summer of 1890, time was running out for the tariff bill to be passed. Many congressmen were up for election in the fall and they were eager to get home and campaign. To get a vote on the tariff, Harrison was going to have to postpone another measure he wanted, the Lodge Election Bill. The purpose of the Lodge bill was to protect the voting rights of blacks in the South. It would provide for officials to supervise voter registration and voting in congressional elections.

The Democratic South was solidly against this bill. They called it the Force Bill and spread the false rumor that the army would be called in to run elections. Part of the South's objection was simple prejudice; part of it was practical. While southern whites were solidly Democratic, southern blacks would probably vote Republican.

The Force Bill was going to bring on a long fight, and Republican leaders did not have a long time. In their eyes, the tariff was more important than the election bill. Republicans decided to postpone voting on the Lodge Election Bill until after the 1890 congressional elections.

On the very last day of the congressional session, Harrison signed the McKinley tariff into law. The Republicans had kept their most important campaign promise, but the tariff worked against them in the elections. Democrats whipped up people's fears that prices would be soaring. In Senator McKinley's home district, they hired peddlers to go through the countryside selling cups, usually worth a nickel, for a dollar. When people objected to the outlandish price, the peddlers blamed the tariff. Then they urged housewives to buy before prices went even higher!

William McKinley

Senator McKinley was not reelected. Although they held on to a narrow majority of eight votes in the Senate, Republicans lost control of the House of Representatives; they held 86 seats to the Democrats' 235. It had been difficult enough to get support for Harrison's program before the election; with the loss of the House, it would be impossible. Although Harrison continued to back the Lodge Election Bill, the House Democrats would never let the bill come to a vote. The intimidation of southern black voters continued without federal interference.

Chapter 8

No Retreat

Harrison turned his attention to foreign affairs. He and Secretary of State Blaine made reciprocity agreements with nine countries, including Brazil and Spain. In spring 1891, Harrison made a 9,000-mile tour across the country, traveling through twenty-two states in a luxurious five-car train. Large crowds waited to see the president at stops all along the way. By the end of the trip, he had made 142 speeches, an average of four a day! On this trip, Harrison learned that Blaine had had a total nervous collapse. The president would have to handle foreign affairs by telegraph for most of his trip.

Harrison's staff was small; the work of correspondence, meetings, and receptions was immense. Harrison counted on his family to help with public receptions and official dinners. Besides Harrison and Carrie, the White House family included Carrie's father and Harrison's married daughter, Mary, and her two children. Mary's son, Benjamin Harrison McKee, was a special favorite whose high chair was usually right beside the president's chair at meals. Harrison's son Russell and his wife and daughter also lived there for part of Harrison's term, as did Carrie's widowed niece, Mary Lord Dimmick.

Harrison's daughter Mary McKee (left), daughter-in-law Mrs. Russell Harrison (center), and their children. At right is favorite grandson Benjamin Harrison McKee.

Other Harrison family members lived at the White House for short times; illness and death burdened Harrison's administration. In 1889, Harrison's executive secretary, Elijah Halford, collapsed at his desk from overwork. Halford was too ill to be moved, so he was nursed back to health at the White House. Benjamin F. Tracy, Harrison's capable secretary of the navy, lost his wife and daughter and was badly burned himself in a house fire in February 1890. Harrison rushed to the fire, gave Tracy artificial respiration, and had him moved into the White House until he recovered from his injuries. Secretary of the Interior John W. Noble was ill for two years. William Windom, the secretary of the treasury, died unexpectedly in January 1891.

James G. Blaine

Secretary of State Blaine was not well when he accepted his appointment. In the first years, he relied on his son Walker to keep him in touch when he was too ill to leave home. When thirty-four-year-old Walker died of pneumonia in January 1890, Blaine was devastated. His own collapse followed in April 1891. Blaine did not resign, but he became increasingly remote, frail, and forgetful.

In foreign affairs, Harrison showed the same directness and impatience with delay that he showed to job-seekers. When Germany led a group of European countries in banning imports of American pork, Blaine recommended giving Germany tariff concessions. Harrison threatened to raise the tariff on German products instead. Harrison's tough stand worked. Germany lifted the ban.

Harrison is shown resolving the Chilean affair with a glorious flourish.

Harrison did not flinch when it looked as if the United States would go to war against Chile in 1892. That year a revolutionary regime hostile to the United States took over the Chilean government. During the unrest, when sailors from an American ship went ashore, they were attacked in a bar by a group that included Chilean police officers. Two Americans died. Chile sent no apology and dismissed it as a drunken brawl. Secretary of State Blaine was willing to compromise, but Harrison was not. In a message to Congress he said, "If the dignity as well as the prestige and influence of the United States are not to be wholly sacrificed, we must protect those who in foreign ports display the flag or wear the colors." Chile apologized.

In these and other matters, Harrison bypassed Blaine. Blaine couldn't help noticing that he no longer directed the nation's foreign policy. He began to resent the president. He was encouraged in his resentment by a group of disenchanted Republicans.

Thomas Platt of New York, Matthew Quay of Pennsylvania, and James Clarkson of Iowa were all influential Republicans. All of them felt they had not been properly rewarded by Harrison, and they were determined to stop him. They did not want him as the Republican presidential candidate in 1892. Instead, they chose the unfailingly popular Blaine. Blaine's broken health did not matter to them; they wanted Harrison out.

Harrison himself did not want to run for a second term, but he did not want to back down to make room for Blaine. On May 21, 1892, less than three weeks before the Republican convention, Harrison told his friends, "No Harrison has ever retreated in the presence of a foe without giving battle, and so I have determined to stand and fight." Three days before the convention, Blaine resigned as secretary of state. Harrison accepted his resignation immediately.

Harrison's friends worked hard in the days before the convention. He was nominated on the first ballot, with 535 votes to Blaine's 182. This was Blaine's last try for the presidency; he died in January 1893.

The Democrats nominated Grover Cleveland. Ordinarily, Harrison would have launched into a speaking campaign, but for this election he did not campaign at all. Most people felt that it was undignified for a president to campaign for himself, but Harrison had reasons of his own. For one thing, pressing business kept him hard at work. For another, Carrie Harrison was dying of tuberculosis. Harrison was too preoccupied with her health to campaign. When Grover Cleveland learned about Mrs. Harrison's condition, he, too, decided not to campaign.

During these hot summer months, steelworkers went on strike against the Carnegie Steel Company in Homestead, Pennsylvania. The owners refused to acknowledge the steelworkers' union and locked out the striking workers. In one fight between the guards and the strikers, twenty men were killed. Publicly, Harrison spoke out against unlawful disorder. Privately he had his friends urge the owners to compromise with the union; it did no good.

There were violent railroad strikes in New York and miners' strikes in Tennessee and Idaho. The effect of this unrest was to turn labor against Harrison and the Republicans. In workers' eyes, the tariff brought larger profits to business but failed to raise wages or improve working conditions. They were ready to vote for Cleveland.

Carrie Harrison died in the White House on October 25, 1892. After a Washington memorial service, family and friends took her body by train to Indianapolis for burial. Harrison made no speeches on this trip. He wrote a letter of public thanks to all who had attended the Indianapolis service: "We yearn to tarry with you and to rest near the hallowed spots where your loving hands have laid our dead; but . . . public business will no longer wait upon my sorrow. May a gracious God keep and bless you all!"

By 3:00 A.M. on election day in 1892, Harrison knew he had lost. Cleveland won 277 electoral votes; Harrison, 145. Cleveland had even carried Harrison's home state of Indiana—partly because at the last minute, Harrison's old Republican rival, Walter Q. Gresham, had thrown his support to Cleveland. Gresham later was named Cleveland's secretary of state.

A White House memorial service for Carrie Harrison

Harrison was defeated by a combination of things. Western states wanted free use of silver coins. Laborers looked on the Republicans as friends of big business. The McKinley tariff had not been in effect long enough to deliver the benefits that had been promised.

Harrison did not seem disappointed. He confided to a friend, "Indeed after the heavy blow the death of my wife dealt me, I do not think I could have stood the strain a re-election would have brought." Cleveland was inaugurated on a cold, snowy day. After the ceremony, Harrison took a train to Indianapolis to resume life as a private citizen. Hundreds of people were waiting to welcome him home. He had been dreading coming back without Carrie, but he said to his son, "I made no mistake in coming home at once—there are no friends like the old ones."

Chapter 9

Senior Statesman

By 1896, the Democrats had lost support; people once again turned to the Republican Party, and Harrison became popular again. Newspapers that had found him a cold president now rediscovered his sense of humor. For Harrison, freedom from the burdens of the presidency made all the difference. "Few of the newspaper writers seem to get on to the fact that a poor ass, that is carrying three loads, cannot expect to be frisky as a led colt."

But Harrison flatly refused to run again. He did consent to make some speeches for the Republican candidate, William McKinley of Ohio. Harrison was still at his best when addressing a crowd, and his speeches won national attention. As one admirer put it, he "can think on his feet and never slop over when he says it."

Harrison found himself in demand as a speaker and a lawyer. He delivered a series of lectures at Stanford University in California and wrote nine articles for the *Ladies' Home Journal*. He accepted legal cases very selectively. He argued Venezuela's side of a territorial dispute before an international tribunal in 1899. He also built a camp in the Adirondack Mountains so that he could spend summers hunting and fishing with his grandchildren.

Much to his children's surprise, Harrison remarried at a small ceremony in New York in 1896. His second wife was Mary Lord Dimmick, Caroline Harrison's niece who had helped nurse her in her illness. Harrison explained to his son, "A home is life's essential to me and it must be the old home. . . . I am sure [my children] will not wish me to live the years that remain to me in solitude." Harrison and his wife had a daughter, Elizabeth, born February 21, 1897.

In March 1901, Harrison caught a cold that turned into pneumonia. Mary Harrison was with him when he died the afternoon of March 13, 1901. While Harrison's body lay in state, the survivors of the 70th Indiana, Harrison's Civil War regiment, led thousands of soldiers in a memorial march. At the funeral, the poet James Whitcomb Riley praised Harrison for "his fearless independence and stand for what he believed to be right and just."

Harrison deserved this praise. He did lead a life of integrity. Perhaps his independence made him a better man than he was a politician. In an age of florid oratory, he spoke directly and relied on facts rather than style to win people to his way of thinking. In an age when political parties wielded power for their own benefit, Harrison maintained an honest administration. He took his campaign promises seriously and did his best to fulfill them. The pattern of his life was a logical one, for it was a life where work and dedication were rewarded. Harrison believed in things—the Republican Party, the Presbyterian Church, the Union cause—and he was willing to commit to them his intelligence, his energy, and even his life.

Opposite page: Harrison weds Mary Lord Dimmick.

Chronology of American History

(Shaded area covers events in Benjamin Harrison's lifetime.)

About A.D. 982 — Eric the Red, born in Norway, reaches Greenland in one of the first European voyages to North America.

About 1000 — Leif Ericson (Eric the Red's son) leads what is thought to be the first European expedition to mainland North America; Leif probably lands in Canada.

1492 — Christopher Columbus, seeking a sea route from Spain to the Far East, discovers the New World.

1497 — John Cabot reaches Canada in the first English voyage to North America.

1513 — Ponce de León explores Florida in search of the fabled Fountain of Youth.

1519-1521 — Hernando Cortés of Spain conquers Mexico.

1534 — French explorers led by Jacques Cartier enter the Gulf of St. Lawrence in Canada.

1540 — Spanish explorer Francisco Coronado begins exploring the American Southwest, seeking the riches of the mythical Seven Cities of Cibola.

1565 — St. Augustine, Florida, the first permanent European town in what is now the United States, is founded by the Spanish.

1607 — Jamestown, Virginia, is founded, the first permanent English town in the present-day U.S.

1608 — Frenchman Samuel de Champlain founds the village of Quebec, Canada.

1609 — Henry Hudson explores the eastern coast of present-day U.S. for the Netherlands; the Dutch then claim parts of New York, New Jersey, Delaware, and Connecticut and name the area New Netherland.

1619 — The English colonies' first shipment of black slaves arrives in Jamestown.

1620 — English Pilgrims found Massachusetts' first permanent town at Plymouth.

1621 — Massachusetts Pilgrims and Indians hold the famous first Thanksgiving feast in colonial America.

1623 — Colonization of New Hampshire is begun by the English.

1624 — Colonization of present-day New York State is begun by the Dutch at Fort Orange (Albany).

1625 — The Dutch start building New Amsterdam (now New York City).

1630 — The town of Boston, Massachusetts, is founded by the English Puritans.

1633 — Colonization of Connecticut is begun by the English.

1634 — Colonization of Maryland is begun by the English.

1636 — Harvard, the colonies' first college, is founded in Massachusetts. Rhode Island colonization begins when Englishman Roger Williams founds Providence.

1638 — Delaware colonization begins as Swedes build Fort Christina at present-day Wilmington.

1640 — Stephen Daye of Cambridge, Massachusetts prints *The Bay Psalm Book*, the first English-language book published in what is now the U.S.

1643 — Swedish settlers begin colonizing Pennsylvania.

About 1650 — North Carolina is colonized by Virginia settlers.

1660 — New Jersey colonization is begun by the Dutch at present-day Jersey City.

1670 — South Carolina colonization is begun by the English near Charleston.

1673 — Jacques Marquette and Louis Jolliet explore the upper Mississippi River for France.

1682 — Philadelphia, Pennsylvania, is settled. La Salle explores Mississippi River all the way to its mouth in Louisiana and claims the whole Mississippi Valley for France.

1693 — College of William and Mary is founded in Williamsburg, Virginia.

1700 — Colonial population is about 250,000.

1703 — Benjamin Franklin is born in Boston.

1732 — George Washington, first president of the U.S., is born in Westmoreland County, Virginia.

1733 — James Oglethorpe founds Savannah, Georgia; Georgia is established as the thirteenth colony.

1735 — John Adams, second president of the U.S., is born in Braintree, Massachusetts.

1737 — William Byrd founds Richmond, Virginia.

1738 — British troops are sent to Georgia over border dispute with Spain.

1739 — Black insurrection takes place in South Carolina.

1740 — English Parliament passes act allowing naturalization of immigrants to American colonies after seven-year residence.

1743 — Thomas Jefferson is born in Albemarle County, Virginia. Benjamin Franklin retires at age thirty-seven to devote himself to scientific inquiries and public service.

1744 — King George's War begins; France joins war effort against England.

1745 — During King George's War, France raids settlements in Maine and New York.

1747 — Classes begin at Princeton College in New Jersey.

1748 — The Treaty of Aix-la-Chapelle concludes King George's War.

1749 — Parliament legally recognizes slavery in colonies and the inauguration of the plantation system in the South. George Washington becomes the surveyor for Culpepper County in Virginia.

1750 — Thomas Walker passes through and names Cumberland Gap on his way toward Kentucky region. Colonial population is about 1,200,000.

1751 — James Madison, fourth president of the U.S., is born in Port Conway, Virginia. English Parliament passes Currency Act, banning New England colonies from issuing paper money. George Washington travels to Barbados.

1752 — Pennsylvania Hospital, the first general hospital in the colonies, is founded in Philadelphia. Benjamin Franklin uses a kite in a thunderstorm to demonstrate that lightning is a form of electricity.

1753 — George Washington delivers command that the French withdraw from the Ohio River Valley; French disregard the demand. Colonial population is about 1,328,000.

1754 — French and Indian War begins (extends to Europe as the Seven Years' War). Washington surrenders at Fort Necessity.

1755 — French and Indians ambush Braddock. Washington becomes commander of Virginia troops.

1756 — England declares war on France.

1758 — James Monroe, fifth president of the U.S., is born in Westmoreland County, Virginia.

1759 — Cherokee Indian war begins in southern colonies; hostilities extend to 1761. George Washington marries Martha Dandridge Custis.

1760 — George III becomes king of England. Colonial population is about 1,600,000.

1762 — England declares war on Spain.

1763 — Treaty of Paris concludes the French and Indian War and the Seven Years' War. England gains Canada and most other French lands east of the Mississippi River.

1764 — British pass the Sugar Act to gain tax money from the colonists. The issue of taxation without representation is first introduced in Boston. John Adams marries Abigail Smith.

1765 — Stamp Act goes into effect in the colonies. Business virtually stops as almost all colonists refuse to use the stamps.

1766 — British repeal the Stamp Act.

1767—John Quincy Adams, sixth president of the U.S. and son of second president John Adams, is born in Braintree, Massachusetts. Andrew Jackson, seventh president of the U.S., is born in Waxhaw settlement, South Carolina.

1769—Daniel Boone sights the Kentucky Territory.

1770—In the Boston Massacre, British soldiers kill five colonists and injure six. Townshend Acts are repealed, thus eliminating all duties on imports to the colonies except tea.

1771—Benjamin Franklin begins his autobiography, a work that he will never complete. The North Carolina assembly passes the "Bloody Act," which makes rioters guilty of treason.

1772—Samuel Adams rouses colonists to consider British threats to self-government.

1773—English Parliament passes the Tea Act. Colonists dressed as Mohawk Indians board British tea ships and toss 342 casks of tea into the water in what becomes known as the Boston Tea Party. William Henry Harrison is born in Charles City County, Virginia.

1774—British close the port of Boston to punish the city for the Boston Tea Party. First Continental Congress convenes in Philadelphia.

1775—American Revolution begins with battles of Lexington and Concord, Massachusetts. Second Continental Congress opens in Philadelphia. George Washington becomes commander-in-chief of the Continental army.

1776—Declaration of Independence is adopted on July 4.

1777—Congress adopts the American flag with thirteen stars and thirteen stripes. John Adams is sent to France to negotiate peace treaty.

1778—France declares war against Great Britain and becomes U.S. ally.

1779—British surrender to Americans at Vincennes. Thomas Jefferson is elected governor of Virginia. James Madison is elected to the Continental Congress.

1780—Benedict Arnold, first American traitor, defects to the British.

1781—Articles of Confederation go into effect. Cornwallis surrenders to George Washington at Yorktown, ending the American Revolution.

1782—American commissioners, including John Adams, sign peace treaty with British in Paris. Thomas Jefferson's wife, Martha, dies. Martin Van Buren is born in Kinderhook, New York.

1784—Zachary Taylor is born near Barboursville, Virginia.

1785—Congress adopts the dollar as the unit of currency. John Adams is made minister to Great Britain. Thomas Jefferson is appointed minister to France.

1786—Shays's Rebellion begins in Massachusetts.

1787—Constitutional Convention assembles in Philadelphia, with George Washington presiding; U.S. Constitution is adopted. Delaware, New Jersey, and Pennsylvania become states.

1788—Virginia, South Carolina, New York, Connecticut, New Hampshire, Maryland, and Massachusetts become states. U.S. Constitution is ratified. New York City is declared U.S. capital.

1789—Presidential electors elect George Washington and John Adams as first president and vice-president. Thomas Jefferson is appointed secretary of state. North Carolina becomes a state. French Revolution begins.

1790—Supreme Court meets for the first time. Rhode Island becomes a state. First national census in the U.S. counts 3,929,214 persons. John Tyler is born in Charles City County, Virginia.

1791—Vermont enters the Union. U.S. Bill of Rights, the first ten amendments to the Constitution, goes into effect. District of Columbia is established. James Buchanan is born in Stony Batter, Pennsylvania.

1792—Thomas Paine publishes *The Rights of Man*. Kentucky becomes a state. Two political parties are formed in the U.S., Federalist and Republican. Washington is elected to a second term, with Adams as vice-president.

1793—War between France and Britain begins; U.S. declares neutrality. Eli Whitney invents the cotton gin; cotton production and slave labor increase in the South.

1794—Eleventh Amendment to the Constitution is passed, limiting federal courts' power. "Whiskey Rebellion" in Pennsylvania protests federal whiskey tax. James Madison marries Dolley Payne Todd.

1795—George Washington signs the Jay Treaty with Great Britain. Treaty of San Lorenzo, between U.S. and Spain, settles Florida boundary and gives U.S. right to navigate the Mississippi. James Polk is born near Pineville, North Carolina.

1796—Tennessee enters the Union. Washington gives his Farewell Address, refusing a third presidential term. John Adams is elected president and Thomas Jefferson vice-president.

1797—Adams recommends defense measures against possible war with France. Napoleon Bonaparte and his army march against Austrians in Italy. U.S. population is about 4,900,000.

1798—Washington is named commander-in-chief of the U.S. Army. Department of the Navy is created. Alien and Sedition Acts are passed. Napoleon's troops invade Egypt and Switzerland.

1799—George Washington dies at Mount Vernon, New York. James Monroe is elected governor of Virginia. French Revolution ends. Napoleon becomes ruler of France.

1800—Thomas Jefferson and Aaron Burr tie for president. U.S. capital is moved from Philadelphia to Washington, D.C. The White House is built as presidents' home. Spain returns Louisiana to France. Millard Fillmore is born in Locke, New York.

1801—After thirty-six ballots, House of Representatives elects Thomas Jefferson president, making Burr vice-president. James Madison is named secretary of state.

1802—Congress abolishes excise taxes. U.S. Military Academy is founded at West Point, New York.

1803—Ohio enters the Union. Louisiana Purchase treaty is signed with France, greatly expanding U.S. territory.

1804—Twelfth Amendment to the Constitution rules that president and vice-president be elected separately. Alexander Hamilton is killed by Vice-President Aaron Burr in a duel. Orleans Territory is established. Napoleon crowns himself emperor of France. Franklin Pierce is born in Hillsborough Lower Village, New Hampshire.

1805—Thomas Jefferson begins his second term as president. Lewis and Clark expedition reaches the Pacific Ocean.

1806—Coinage of silver dollars is stopped; resumes in 1836.

1807—Aaron Burr is acquitted in treason trial. Embargo Act closes U.S. ports to trade.

1808—James Madison is elected president. Congress outlaws importing slaves from Africa. Andrew Johnson is born in Raleigh, North Carolina.

1809—Abraham Lincoln is born near Hodgenville, Kentucky.

1810—U.S. population is 7,240,000.

1811—William Henry Harrison defeats Indians at Tippecanoe. Monroe is named secretary of state.

1812—Louisiana becomes a state. U.S. declares war on Britain (War of 1812). James Madison is reelected president. Napoleon invades Russia.

1813—British forces take Fort Niagara and Buffalo, New York.

1814—Francis Scott Key writes "The Star-Spangled Banner." British troops burn much of Washington, D.C., including the White House. Treaty of Ghent ends War of 1812. James Monroe becomes secretary of war.

1815—Napoleon meets his final defeat at Battle of Waterloo.

1816—James Monroe is elected president. Indiana becomes a state.

1817—Mississippi becomes a state. Construction on Erie Canal begins.

1818—Illinois enters the Union. The present thirteen-stripe flag is adopted. Border between U.S. and Canada is agreed upon.

1819—Alabama becomes a state. U.S. purchases Florida from Spain. Thomas Jefferson establishes the University of Virginia.

1820—James Monroe is reelected. In the Missouri Compromise, Maine enters the Union as a free (non-slave) state.

1821—Missouri enters the Union as a slave state. Santa Fe Trail opens the American Southwest. Mexico declares independence from Spain. Napoleon Bonaparte dies.

1822—U.S. recognizes Mexico and Colombia. Liberia in Africa is founded as a home for freed slaves. Ulysses S. Grant is born in Point Pleasant, Ohio. Rutherford B. Hayes is born in Delaware, Ohio.

1823—Monroe Doctrine closes North and South America to European colonizing or invasion.

1824—House of Representatives elects John Quincy Adams president when none of the four candidates wins a majority in national election. Mexico becomes a republic.

1825—Erie Canal is opened. U.S. population is 11,300,000.

1826—Thomas Jefferson and John Adams both die on July 4, the fiftieth anniversary of the Declaration of Independence.

1828—Andrew Jackson is elected president. Tariff of Abominations is passed, cutting imports.

1829—James Madison attends Virginia's constitutional convention. Slavery is abolished in Mexico. Chester A. Arthur is born in Fairfield, Vermont.

1830—Indian Removal Act to resettle Indians west of the Mississippi is approved.

1831—James Monroe dies in New York City. James A. Garfield is born in Orange, Ohio. Cyrus McCormick develops his reaper.

1832—Andrew Jackson, nominated by the new Democratic Party, is reelected president.

1833—Britain abolishes slavery in its colonies. Benjamin Harrison is born in North Bend, Ohio.

1835—Federal government becomes debt-free for the first time.

1836—Martin Van Buren becomes president. Texas wins independence from Mexico. Arkansas joins the Union. James Madison dies at Montpelier, Virginia.

1837—Michigan enters the Union. U.S. population is 15,900,000. Grover Cleveland is born in Caldwell, New Jersey.

1840—William Henry Harrison is elected president.

1841—President Harrison dies in Washington, D.C., one month after inauguration. Vice-President John Tyler succeeds him.

1843—William McKinley is born in Niles, Ohio.

1844—James Knox Polk is elected president. Samuel Morse sends first telegraphic message.

1845—Texas and Florida become states. Potato famine in Ireland causes massive emigration from Ireland to U.S. Andrew Jackson dies near Nashville, Tennessee.

1846—Iowa enters the Union. War with Mexico begins.

1847—U.S. captures Mexico City.

1848—John Quincy Adams dies in Washington, D.C. Zachary Taylor becomes president. Treaty of Guadalupe Hidalgo ends Mexico-U.S. war. Wisconsin becomes a state.

1849—James Polk dies in Nashville, Tennessee.

1850—President Taylor dies in Washington, D.C.; Vice-President Millard Fillmore succeeds him. California enters the Union, breaking tie between slave and free states.

1852—Franklin Pierce is elected president.

1853—Gadsden Purchase transfers Mexican territory to U.S.

1854—"War for Bleeding Kansas" is fought between slave and free states.

1855—Czar Nicholas I of Russia dies, succeeded by Alexander II.

1856—James Buchanan is elected president. In Massacre of Potawatomi Creek, Kansas-slavers are murdered by free-staters. Woodrow Wilson is born in Staunton, Virginia.

1857—William Howard Taft is born in Cincinnati, Ohio.

1858—Minnesota enters the Union. Theodore Roosevelt is born in New York City.

1859—Oregon becomes a state.

1860—Abraham Lincoln is elected president; South Carolina secedes from the Union in protest.

1861—Arkansas, Tennessee, North Carolina, and Virginia secede. Kansas enters the Union as a free state. Civil War begins.

1862—Union forces capture Fort Henry, Roanoke Island, Fort Donelson, Jacksonville, and New Orleans; Union armies are defeated at the battles of Bull Run and Fredericksburg. Martin Van Buren dies in Kinderhook, New York. John Tyler dies near Charles City, Virginia.

1863—Lincoln issues Emancipation Proclamation: all slaves held in rebelling territories are declared free. West Virginia becomes a state.

1864—Abraham Lincoln is reelected. Nevada becomes a state.

1865—Lincoln is assassinated in Washington, D.C., and succeeded by Andrew Johnson. U.S. Civil War ends on May 26. Thirteenth Amendment abolishes slavery. Warren G. Harding is born in Blooming Grove, Ohio.

1867—Nebraska becomes a state. U.S. buys Alaska from Russia for $7,200,000. Reconstruction Acts are passed.

1868—President Johnson is impeached for violating Tenure of Office Act, but is acquitted by Senate. Ulysses S. Grant is elected president. Fourteenth Amendment prohibits voting discrimination. James Buchanan dies in Lancaster, Pennsylvania.

1869—Franklin Pierce dies in Concord, New Hampshire.

1870—Fifteenth Amendment gives blacks the right to vote.

1872—Grant is reelected over Horace Greeley. General Amnesty Act pardons ex-Confederates. Calvin Coolidge is born in Plymouth Notch, Vermont.

1874—Millard Fillmore dies in Buffalo, New York. Herbert Hoover is born in West Branch, Iowa.

1875—Andrew Johnson dies in Carter's Station, Tennessee.

1876—Colorado enters the Union. "Custer's last stand": he and his men are massacred by Sioux Indians at Little Big Horn, Montana.

1877—Rutherford B. Hayes is elected president as all disputed votes are awarded to him.

1880—James A. Garfield is elected president.

1881—President Garfield is assassinated and dies in Elberon, New Jersey. Vice-President Chester A. Arthur succeeds him.

1882—U.S. bans Chinese immigration. Franklin D. Roosevelt is born in Hyde Park, New York.

1884—Grover Cleveland is elected president. Harry S. Truman is born in Lamar, Missouri.

1885—Ulysses S. Grant dies in Mount McGregor, New York.

1886—Statue of Liberty is dedicated. Chester A. Arthur dies in New York City.

1888—Benjamin Harrison is elected president.

1889—North Dakota, South Dakota, Washington, and Montana become states.

1890—Dwight D. Eisenhower is born in Denison, Texas. Idaho and Wyoming become states.

1892—Grover Cleveland is elected president.

1893—Rutherford B. Hayes dies in Fremont, Ohio.

1896—William McKinley is elected president. Utah becomes a state.

1898—U.S. declares war on Spain over Cuba.

1900—McKinley is reelected. Boxer Rebellion against foreigners in China begins.

1901—McKinley is assassinated by anarchist Leon Czolgosz in Buffalo, New York; Theodore Roosevelt becomes president. Benjamin Harrison dies in Indianapolis, Indiana.

1902—U.S. acquires perpetual control over Panama Canal.

1903—Alaskan frontier is settled.

1904—Russian-Japanese War breaks out. Theodore Roosevelt wins presidential election.

1905—Treaty of Portsmouth signed, ending Russian-Japanese War.

1906—U.S. troops occupy Cuba.

1907—President Roosevelt bars all Japanese immigration. Oklahoma enters the Union.

1908—William Howard Taft becomes president. Grover Cleveland dies in Princeton, New Jersey. Lyndon B. Johnson is born near Stonewall, Texas.

1909—NAACP is founded under W.E.B. DuBois

1910—China abolishes slavery.

1911—Chinese Revolution begins. Ronald Reagan is born in Tampico, Illinois.

1912—Woodrow Wilson is elected president. Arizona and New Mexico become states.

1913—Federal income tax is introduced in U.S. through the Sixteenth Amendment. Richard Nixon is born in Yorba Linda, California. Gerald Ford is born in Omaha, Nebraska.

1914—World War I begins.

1915—British liner *Lusitania* is sunk by German submarine.

1916—Wilson is reelected president.

1917—U.S. breaks diplomatic relations with Germany. Czar Nicholas of Russia abdicates as revolution begins. U.S. declares war on Austria-Hungary. John F. Kennedy is born in Brookline, Massachusetts.

1918—Wilson proclaims "Fourteen Points" as war aims. On November 11, armistice is signed between Allies and Germany.

1919—Eighteenth Amendment prohibits sale and manufacture of intoxicating liquors. Wilson presides over first League of Nations; wins Nobel Peace Prize. Theodore Roosevelt dies in Oyster Bay, New York.

1920—Nineteenth Amendment (women's suffrage) is passed. Warren Harding is elected president.

1921—Adolf Hitler's stormtroopers begin to terrorize political opponents.

1922—Irish Free State is established. Soviet states form USSR. Benito Mussolini forms Fascist government in Italy.

1923—President Harding dies in San Francisco, California; he is succeeded by Vice-President Calvin Coolidge.

1924—Coolidge is elected president. Woodrow Wilson dies in Washington, D.C. James Carter is born in Plains, Georgia. George Bush is born in Milton, Massachusetts.

1925—Hitler reorganizes Nazi Party and publishes first volume of *Mein Kampf.*

1926—Fascist youth organizations founded in Germany and Italy. Republic of Lebanon proclaimed.

1927—Stalin becomes Soviet dictator. Economic conference in Geneva attended by fifty-two nations.

1928—Herbert Hoover is elected president. U.S. and many other nations sign Kellogg-Briand pacts to outlaw war.

1929—Stock prices in New York crash on "Black Thursday"; the Great Depression begins.

1930—Bank of U.S. and its many branches close (most significant bank failure of the year). William Howard Taft dies in Washington, D.C.

1931—Emigration from U.S. exceeds immigration for first time as Depression deepens.

1932—Franklin D. Roosevelt wins presidential election in a Democratic landslide.

1933—First concentration camps are erected in Germany. U.S. recognizes USSR and resumes trade. Twenty-First Amendment repeals prohibition. Calvin Coolidge dies in Northampton, Massachusetts.

1934—Severe dust storms hit Plains states. President Roosevelt passes U.S. Social Security Act.

1936—Roosevelt is reelected. Spanish Civil War begins. Hitler and Mussolini form Rome-Berlin Axis.

1937—Roosevelt signs Neutrality Act.

1938—Roosevelt sends appeal to Hitler and Mussolini to settle European problems amicably.

1939—Germany takes over Czechoslovakia and invades Poland, starting World War II.

1940—Roosevelt is reelected for a third term.

1941—Japan bombs Pearl Harbor, U.S. declares war on Japan. Germany and Italy declare war on U.S.; U.S. then declares war on them.

1942—Allies agree not to make separate peace treaties with the enemies. U.S. government transfers more than 100,000 Nisei (Japanese-Americans) from west coast to inland concentration camps.

1943—Allied bombings of Germany begin.

1944—Roosevelt is reelected for a fourth term. Allied forces invade Normandy on D-Day.

1945—President Franklin D. Roosevelt dies in Warm Springs, Georgia; Vice-President Harry S. Truman succeeds him. Mussolini is killed; Hitler commits suicide. Germany surrenders. U.S. drops atomic bomb on Hiroshima; Japan surrenders: end of World War II.

1946—U.N. General Assembly holds its first session in London. Peace conference of twenty-one nations is held in Paris.

1947—Peace treaties are signed in Paris. "Cold War" is in full swing.

1948—U.S. passes Marshall Plan Act, providing $17 billion in aid for Europe. U.S. recognizes new nation of Israel. India and Pakistan become free of British rule. Truman is elected president.

1949—Republic of Eire is proclaimed in Dublin. Russia blocks land route access from Western Germany to Berlin; airlift begins. U.S., France, and Britain agree to merge their zones of occupation in West Germany. Apartheid program begins in South Africa.

1950—Riots in Johannesburg, South Africa, against apartheid. North Korea invades South Korea. U.N. forces land in South Korea and recapture Seoul.

1951—Twenty-Second Amendment limits president to two terms.

1952—Dwight D. Eisenhower resigns as supreme commander in Europe and is elected president.

1953—Stalin dies; struggle for power in Russia follows. Rosenbergs are executed for espionage.

1954—U.S. and Japan sign mutual defense agreement.

1955—Blacks in Montgomery, Alabama, boycott segregated bus lines.

1956—Eisenhower is reelected president. Soviet troops march into Hungary.

1957—U.S. agrees to withdraw ground forces from Japan. Russia launches first satellite, *Sputnik.*

1958—European Common Market comes into being. Fidel Castro begins war against Batista government in Cuba.

1959—Alaska becomes the forty-ninth state. Hawaii becomes fiftieth state. Castro becomes premier of Cuba. De Gaulle is proclaimed president of the Fifth Republic of France.

1960—Historic debates between Senator John F. Kennedy and Vice-President Richard Nixon are televised. Kennedy is elected president. Brezhnev becomes president of USSR.

1961—Berlin Wall is constructed. Kennedy and Khrushchev confer in Vienna. In Bay of Pigs incident, Cubans trained by CIA attempt to overthrow Castro.

1962—U.S. military council is established in South Vietnam.

1963—Riots and beatings by police and whites mark civil rights demonstrations in Birmingham, Alabama; 30,000 troops are called out, Martin Luther King, Jr., is arrested. Freedom marchers descend on Washington, D.C., to demonstrate. President Kennedy is assassinated in Dallas, Texas; Vice-President Lyndon B. Johnson is sworn in as president.

1964—U.S. aircraft bomb North Vietnam. Johnson is elected president. Herbert Hoover dies in New York City.

1965—U.S. combat troops arrive in South Vietnam.

1966—Thousands protest U.S. policy in Vietnam. National Guard quells race riots in Chicago.

1967—Six-Day War between Israel and Arab nations.

1968—Martin Luther King, Jr., is assassinated in Memphis, Tennessee. Senator Robert Kennedy is assassinated in Los Angeles. Riots and police brutality take place at Democratic National Convention in Chicago. Richard Nixon is elected president. Czechoslovakia is invaded by Soviet troops.

1969—Dwight D. Eisenhower dies in Washington, D.C. Hundreds of thousands of people in several U.S. cities demonstrate against Vietnam War.

1970—Four Vietnam War protesters are killed by National Guardsmen at Kent State University in Ohio.

1971—Twenty-Sixth Amendment allows eighteen-year-olds to vote.

1972—Nixon visits Communist China; is reelected president in near-record landslide. Watergate affair begins when five men are arrested in the Watergate hotel complex in Washington, D.C. Nixon announces resignations of aides Haldeman, Ehrlichman, and Dean and Attorney General Kleindienst as a result of Watergate-related charges. Harry S. Truman dies in Kansas City, Missouri.

1973—Vice-President Spiro Agnew resigns; Gerald Ford is named vice-president. Vietnam peace treaty is formally approved after nineteen months of negotiations. Lyndon B. Johnson dies in San Antonio, Texas.

1974—As a result of Watergate cover-up, impeachment is considered; Nixon resigns and Ford becomes president. Ford pardons Nixon and grants limited amnesty to Vietnam War draft evaders and military deserters.

1975—U.S. civilians are evacuated from Saigon, South Vietnam, as Communist forces complete takeover of South Vietnam.

1976—U.S. celebrates its Bicentennial. James Earl Carter becomes president.

1977—Carter pardons most Vietnam draft evaders, numbering some 10,000.

1980—Ronald Reagan is elected president.

1981—President Reagan is shot in the chest in assassination attempt. Sandra Day O'Connor is appointed first woman justice of the Supreme Court.

1983—U.S. troops invade island of Grenada.

1984—Reagan is reelected president. Democratic candidate Walter Mondale's running mate, Geraldine Ferraro, is the first woman selected for vice-president by a major U.S. political party.

1985—Soviet Communist Party secretary Konstantin Chernenko dies; Mikhail Gorbachev succeeds him. U.S. and Soviet officials discuss arms control in Geneva. Reagan and Gorbachev hold summit conference in Geneva. Racial tensions accelerate in South Africa.

1986—Space shuttle *Challenger* explodes shortly after takeoff; crew of seven dies. U.S. bombs bases in Libya. Corazon Aquino defeats Ferdinand Marcos in Philippine presidential election.

1987—Iraqi missile rips the U.S. frigate *Stark* in the Persian Gulf, killing thirty-seven American sailors. Congress holds hearings to investigate sale of U.S. arms to Iran to finance Nicaraguan *contra* movement.

1988—President Reagan and Soviet leader Gorbachev sign INF treaty, eliminating intermediate nuclear forces. Severe drought sweeps the United States. George Bush is elected president.

1989—East Germany opens Berlin Wall, allowing citizens free exit. Communists lose control of governments in Poland, Romania, and Czechoslovakia. Chinese troops massacre over 1,000 pro-democracy student demonstrators in Beijing's Tiananmen Square.

1990—Iraq annexes Kuwait, provoking the threat of war. East and West Germany are reunited. The Cold War between the United States and the Soviet Union comes to a close. Several Soviet republics make moves toward independence.

1991—Backed by a coalition of members of the United Nations, U.S. troops drive Iraqis from Kuwait. Latvia, Lithuania, and Estonia withdraw from the USSR. The Soviet Union dissolves as its republics secede to form a Commonwealth of Independent States.

1992—U.N. forces fail to stop fighting in territories of former Yugoslavia. More than fifty people are killed and more than six hundred buildings burned in rioting in Los Angeles. U.S. unemployment reaches eight-year high. Hurricane Andrew devastates southern Florida and parts of Louisiana. International relief supplies and troops are sent to combat famine and violence in Somalia.

1993—U.S.-led forces use airplanes and missiles to attack military targets in Iraq. William Jefferson Clinton becomes the forty-second U.S. president.

1994—Richard M. Nixon dies in New York City.

Index

Page numbers in boldface type indicate illustrations.

About the Author

Susan Clinton holds a Ph.D. in English and is a part-time teacher of English Literature at Northwestern University in Chicago. Her articles have appeared in such publications as *Consumer's Digest*, *Family Style Magazine*, and the Chicago *Reader*. In addition, she has contributed biographical and historical articles to *Encyclopaedia Britannica* and *Compton's Encyclopedia*, and has written reader stories and other materials for a number of educational publishers. Ms. Clinton lives in Chicago with her husband, Pat, and their two boys.